STRENGTHEN YOUR FICTION BY UNDERSTANDING WEASEL WORDS

WEASEL WORDS CATEGORIZED BY THE PROBLEMS THEY INDICATE AND HOW TO FIND THEM WITH ONE CLICK

MELISSA JAGEARS

CONTENTS

PART 1
WHAT ARE WEASEL WORDS?

1. Unneeded Weasel Words — 7
2. Clustered Weasel Words — 14
3. Grammar Weasel Words — 21
4. To Be Weasel Words — 30
5. Vague and Confusing Weasel Words — 35
6. POV-Distancing Weasel Words — 40

PART 2
SETTING UP YOUR SOFTWARE TO FIND WEASEL WORDS

7. Setting Up Word to Find Weasel Words — 55
8. Setting up Open Office to Find Weasel Words — 62
9. Setting up Scrivener to Find Weasel Words — 68

PART 3
PURCHASE AND UPLOAD THE CODE OR TEMPLATE

10. Word Macro Code Uploading Instructions — 77
11. Open Office Macro Code Uploading Instructions — 80
12. Scrivener Template Uploading Instructions — 84

Writing Craft Terms — 87
Acknowledgments — 91
About the Author — 93
Also by Melissa Jagears — 95

PART 1

WHAT ARE WEASEL WORDS?

At some point in your fiction writing career, you've likely come across the term 'weasel words.' If not, you will. Writers use the term 'weasel words' to mean words a writer can eliminate to improve their writing.

However, when I first started writing, every weasel word list I came across was different. And not only were they different, but some weasel words seemed to behave differently.

For example, almost every weasel word list includes the word 'just.' Eliminating 'just' from a sentence trims your word count:

> Example: *I **just** can't wait to leave.*
>
> Fix: *I can't wait to leave.*

But 'was' also appears on these lists, and you can't always cut 'was' out:

> Example: *He **was** sore.*
>
> Cannot become: *He sore.*

So what should a writer do with the weasel word 'was'? Is 'was' even a weasel word?

When I was learning to write, I collected all the weasel words writers suggested ought to be cut and sifted through them. I tried to discover why writers bothered to search out weasel words since eradicating them without thought would result in my writing sounding stilted or nonsensical.

I soon realized not all weasel words indicate places to trim word count. Sometimes they serve to indicate writing craft problems, and fixing those problems might actually *add* to the story's word count. Correcting these issues can strengthen a story by enhancing the fictive dream (See Writing Craft Terms at the end of this book) that authors want to immerse their readers in.

Since searching for weasel words can help authors catch storytelling weaknesses, it's a handy way to self-edit. Knowing the rules that govern different types of weasel words will help you decide whether or not something needs fixed.

Once I figured out the underlying problems particular weasel words indicated, I categorized the words and expanded the lists to help me self-edit my fiction. (I only search out weasel words that make a decent impact on my writing. A few other types of weasel words can invade writing, but I won't discuss them in this book. Searching for them isn't worth my time when it will do nothing but cut ten or twenty words from a manuscript.)

In each section of this book, I will explain what writing weakness each type of weasel word indicates and give examples on when to remove those weasel words and when to leave them alone. Sometimes an unnecessary weasel word should remain in the story to prevent pacing, rhythm, characterization, voice, or ambiance problems.

Don't let the rules and lists paralyze you. Don't get stuck agonizing over every weasel word you find. Instead, recognize that weasel words can help you find weaknesses in your writing, but also know that excising all the weasel words can hamper the sound and rhythm of your voice. Learn the reasoning behind the rules, but don't let following the rules steal the breath from your story.

Since this is a book about weasel words, any I use will likely pop out at you. You might be tempted to go, "Aha! She doesn't follow her own rules!" And you're right. Sometimes I break them, often because following a rule keeps it from sounding like me, but I make that conscious decision...and sometimes those weasel words just plain sneak back in. I don't want my manuscript to be bloated with them, so I check them.

You might find you like my example sentences better than my fixes. Since your voice is different than mine, such differences of opinion are perfectly acceptable. Let the rules hone your work, not cripple your voice.

It's not necessary to stop writing your first draft to deal with weasel words, but the more you learn to recognize them and deal with them in editing, the more you'll quit using them in your drafts.

Many weasel words fall into multiple categories, so don't be surprised to see a weasel word in one category and realize it's also causing a problem in another.

At the end of this book, I will show you how to search for weasel words in groups so you can deal with one list at a time with a single click of a button. This way you won't lose editing time clicking the "Find" button over and over again. Word's and Open Office's macro capabilities and Scrivener's search collections make this easy.

If you've never heard of a macro or a search collection, don't despair. I will lead you step-by-step through the macro and search collection building process. They do take a few hours to set up, but you can purchase the macro codes or Scrivener template from me if you'd prefer I do the work for you. Either way, once finished with this book, you'll be able to use weasel words to help you self-edit with just a click of a button.

If you choose to set up the macros or Scrivener template yourself, I provide tips to help you set up the search mechanisms at the end of many weasel word sections. These tips should make your weasel word editing easy.

Now, let's get to the different types of weasel words and see how each should be handled.

> *Caveat*: *I write fiction in the past tense so my weasel word lists contain past tense verbs. If you write in the present tense, you will need to change your verbs to present tense. You might choose to include both tenses if you write in both or write in past tense but use a lot of direct thought in present. The codes and templates I make available for purchase contain both tenses and third person pronouns.*

*If you cannot access the hyperlinks to outside sources, they are available on my website's page for this book.

http://www.melissajagears.com/weasel-words

CHAPTER 1
UNNEEDED WEASEL WORDS

THE FIRST SET of weasel words we'll look at are the easiest to deal with. These words are weasels because they tend to add nothing to your story but word count. Most of the time, your sentence will work fine without these words. However, you don't want to eradicate them without thought. Sometimes you might want to keep them for reasons I will explain.

UNNEEDED WEASELS

The words and phrases that often don't add anything to a story but word count are:

a bit, a number of, about, actual, again, all, almost, already, also, any, anyway, be able to, began, close, enough, even, ever, example of, fairly, far, few, in his/her/my opinion, in order to, just, kind of, like, lot of, many, maybe, most, mostly, often, one of, only, own, particular, pretty, quite, rather, reached out, real, really, several, so,

some, somehow, somewhat, sort of, specific, started, still, sure, that, then, type of, uh, um, various, vast, very, well, whole

These words often add nothing of substance, but don't delete them sight unseen. Sometimes these words are necessary. Even if they aren't, there are reasons to keep weasel words, such as for a particular character's speech tic, adding clarification, or their existence affects the rhythm of the sentence. But most of the time, if the weasel word can be deleted, it's best to do so.

If you're unsure, delete. When you reread your draft, if the word screams to be put back in or the meaning of the sentence has changed, add the word back in.

If having to search out all the weasel words in this list feels daunting—and it is—don't worry. Remember, at the end of this book, I will teach you how to set up your writing software to highlight an entire group of words with one click.

Here are example sentences with unneeded weasels that should be deleted. Deletion may require some rewriting:

> Example: *"A hot cocoa with **some** cinnamon would be nice, if you don't mind."*
>
> Fix: *"A hot cocoa with cinnamon would be nice, if you don't mind."*
>
> Example: *He needed something flat **in order to** pick the lock.*
>
> Fix: *He needed something flat to pick the lock.*

Example: *She wrapped her arm around mine and tugged **a bit**.*

Fix: *She wrapped her arm around mine and tugged.*

Example: *"If you don't want to take the book, **just** borrow it and return it later."*

Fix: *"If you don't want to take the book, borrow it and return it later."*

Example: *They **only** had fifteen minutes left to win.*

Fix: *They had fifteen minutes left to win.*

Example: *He **reached out** to pull her back.*

Fix: *He pulled her back.*

Example: *He **started to** walk down the road.*

Fix: *He walked down the road.*

*The only time you need 'started to' or 'began to' is when the literal start of something is important to the action. I'll have an example later.

Example: ***Many** firefighters rushed to the scene.*

Fix: *Firefighters rushed to the scene.* Or *Twenty firefighters rushed to the scene.*

Example: *I saw **that** you opened the safe.*

Fix: *I saw you opened the safe.*

Example: *Her hair was **very** long.*

Fix: *Her hair fell to the middle of her back.*

* 'Very' is necessary to tell the reader that her hair is longer than normal, and yet, 'very' does little to tell us how long it is. Replacing 'very' and describing/showing is better.

Don't forget, finding an unneeded weasel word in your manuscript doesn't mean you have to eliminate it. Some new writers are afraid that if they find a weasel word, they have to delete or rewrite, but that's not necessarily true. Some unneeded weasel words are almost always unnecessary (e.g. 'just' or 'in order to'), and some are often required (e. g. 'that'). Determine if your weasel words should be removed on a case-by-case basis.

Here are a few examples for when it isn't necessary to rewrite or delete:

Example: *I want to pay for **some** of the tickets.*

Example: *They needed love and care **just** the same.*

*These sentences don't maintain the same meaning or feeling if you delete the weasel word. There may be a way to rewrite (e.g. *I want to pay for three of the tickets.*), but it may not improve the story.

Example: *If only Lydia knew **that** Caroline accusing her of vanity was closer to the mark.*

*This sentence will work grammatically without 'that,' yet the reader might initially read it with the wrong meaning—thinking the sentence is talking about Lydia knowing a person—and so the farther they read, the more they might grow confused and end up needing to reread to understand the sentence. Ease of reading is an important factor to consider when deciding whether or not to delete weasel words.

>Example: *He looked at his wife. "You might think her **pretty**, but she ain't."*

*'Pretty' is not an unnecessary qualifier in this instance. You could use a synonym, but it may not improve anything unless you like the synonym better for the character's voice.

>Example: *If **only** he'd leave her alone, she could work.*

*You could rewrite this as: "If he'd leave her alone, she could work." But the character's frustration would not come through without the 'only.' Keeping this weasel word would be a deep point of view (POV) choice. (See terms)

>Example: ***So many** things were going awry.*

*These two words would be a character's voice choice. You could rewrite as, "Things were going awry." But it loses the exasperation of your character's voice.

>Example: *The band **started to** play, so he had to rush to the floor before Gerald could ask Lily to dance.*

* 'Started to' is necessary so the sentence doesn't read as if anytime your character hears a song, he has to dance with Lily.

BODY PART ACTION WEASELS

Certain actions require certain body parts to move, so pairing the body part with the action verb is redundant. Writing that characters "nodded their heads" is not necessary because what else would they nod?

Many non-body part phrases fall under this rule too, such as 'seven a.m. in the morning,' but they're rarer and not common enough to search for. Nevertheless, keep your eye out for them, as well as for redundant phrases like these:

blinked (**eyes**)
(eyes) **gazed**
clapped (his/her **hands**)
waved (**hand**)
kicked (something with his **foot**)
nodded (**head** and/or **in agreement**)
took/put (**hat**) off/on (**head**)
pointed (**finger**)
shrugged (**shoulders**)
sped up/**slowed** (his/her **pace**)
stood (to their **feet**)
a chuckle/breath/laugh **left**/**escaped** (**mouth**/**lips**)
(**ears**/**nose**) **caught** the (**sound**/**smell**)
(sound/smell) **found** (ears/nose)

Example: *He took his **hat** off his **head** when he stepped into her office.*

Fix: *He took his hat off when he stepped into her office.*

Example: *The wonderful smells **found** their way to his **nose**.*

Fix: *The aroma of basil and garlic wafted from the kitchen.*

*Readers don't need to know these scents are found by the nose. They already know noses smell scents.

Tip for dealing with Unneeded Weasel Words:
If the sentence works without the word, discard it.

Bonus Writing Tip:
If the story works without the scene, discard it.

Hint for the search:

In looking for body part weasels, I highlight the verb in one color and the body part in a different color. That way, I can scan a manuscript for the two colors close together to see if I've used an unnecessary body part weasel.

CHAPTER 2

CLUSTERED WEASEL WORDS

USING the words in the following section is not wrong, but they can become a problem when clumped together.

You may have heard of having echoes (see terms) in your writing. This is when you have a repeated word used so closely together that its usage rings out in the reader's mind, bringing attention to the author's word choice and pulling the reader out of the fictive dream.

Words like 'parsimonious' or 'cacophony,' if used more than once a book, will call attention to themselves. Less unusual words like 'nary' or 'onward' will also stick out if used too many times or close together. Even more common words or phrases like 'moving through' will stand out if they are within a few sentences of each other.

These unusual vocabulary echoes can't be found in a search and replace, but it is something to keep in mind while reading your book.

You could use the word frequency tool in Scrivener or the online Word Frequency Counter at Write Words to look for anything unusual. However, writers use some words often enough that they can clump together easily. Searching for these clustered weasels can help you avoid echoes and highlight places to vary your word choices.

PET WEASELS

My particular pet weasels may not affect other writers, but many do. I also tend to have a new pet word or phrase I seem to be in love with in each new manuscript.

Pet weasels are perfectly acceptable to use often in a book, but when you have too many bunched together, they "echo." I try to keep pet weasels to a minimum. For example, I only let one character smile or use "oh" per several pages—unless it's truly necessary to have more. If I can take them all out of the chapter, the better.

But pet weasels can be hard for writers to spot in their own manuscripts. Sometimes editors won't pick up on them either. You and your editor are often so busy fixing character or plot issues that your heroine biting her lip forty times in a manuscript slides past undetected. However, readers notice since they're devouring the story.

It's a good idea to search for pet weasels to make sure you don't overuse them. If you have personal pet weasels or discover a new pet weasel, add it to the list below:

bit (lip), eyes, gaze, grin, hands on **(hips), looked, narrowed (eyes), nodded, oh, perhaps, quirked,** raised **(brows), seemed, shook (head), shrugged, sighed, smiled, swallowed, Well**

Example:

She **sighed**, **looking** at the teen. "Come on, John."

The young man **shook** his head. "I'm not going."

"Yes, you are."

He put his **hands on** his hips. "Make me."

"**Oh**?" She took a step back and **raised** a brow. "You think I won't?"

He **shrugged**. "**Well**, you never have before."

She **shook** her head. "**Well**, there's a first time for everything."

*In the above scene, I suggest that one of the 'shook head' phrases and one 'well' should be removed at minimum. But I'd also see if I could replace all of them with something better, since these words come in handy while storytelling and will appear often in a manuscript. Replacing these words will also give the scene more interest because pet weasels are what we use when we're writing what comes easiest.

Fix:

She jerked her head toward the door. "Come on, John."

The teen puffed up his chest. "I'm not going.

"Yes, you are."

"Make me." His lips twisted into a sneer.

"**Oh**?" She took a step back and cocked her shoulders. "You think I won't?"

The defiant tilt of his chin descended just a touch. "You never have before."

> She pressed her lips into a tight line. This argument would end now. "There's a first time for everything."

Was it necessary to take out all those pet weasels? Since many showed up only once in the section, they weren't echoes. But it sure made me think harder on how to show the same images and feelings while adding variety to the scene.

Taking a workshop on body language, or reading a book and watching videos on the topic can help you add variety if you're stumped on what to do physically with your characters. Margie Lawson's Writing Body Language workshop is highly recommended.

So even if your Pet Weasels aren't echoing on the page, searching for them will help you find places you can rewrite to better show what's happening in the story.

Hint for the search:

At the end of this book, I will teach you how to highlight weasels in different colors in Word and Open Office. (Unfortunately, Scrivener won't highlight in different colors.) Multiple colors will help you see where you have too many of the same words clumped together.

When searching for these, you might consider looking for 'hips' instead of 'hands on,' or 'brows' over 'raised' etc. to keep your search narrowed to the less common word in the problematic phrases.

Also, consider searching out different iterations of pet weasels, like 'lip' and 'lips.' Don't just search out 'lip' and leave the command for "whole word search" unchecked (which I'll discuss later), because you'll end up highlighting words you don't need to check like 'liposuction' or 'flip.'

PRONOUN CLUSTER WEASELS

Pronouns are not weasels in and of themselves. But when they are clumped together, they can echo on the page. Besides, a lot of 'he's and 'she's together can be confusing.

> **he, she** (for third person point of view), **I** (for first person point of view)

> Example:
>
> *Why was **she** still single? **She**'d given him the impression **she** taught because **she** needed to, not from some higher calling or insatiable desire.*
>
> Fix:
>
> *Why was **she** still single? **He**'d gotten the impression **she** taught out of necessity, not from some higher calling or insatiable desire.*

*In taking out a few 'she's, I got rid of the repetitive echoes and shushing sounds. (If you plan to have an audio version of your book, taking out the shushing is a mighty good idea.)

I also search for 'She' and 'He' (along with my main characters' names) to catch where I have repeated sentences and paragraphs starting with the same pronoun.

> Example:
>
> ***She moved** to the counter. "I'll get that whiskey for you."*

He *followed. "I don't drink."*

She *looked over her shoulder. "You don't? Aren't you a cowboy?"*

He *rolled his eyes. "Drinking isn't required to be a cowboy."*

She *looked him up and down. "Seems muscles and a decent pair of chaps aren't either."*

Fix: (combo of rearranging, rewriting, and differentiating sentence structures)

"I'll get that whiskey for you." Sidestepping him, she sashayed toward the counter.

Why did everyone offer him booze first thing? "I don't drink."

She *looked over her shoulder. "You don't? Aren't you a cowboy?"*

Why was choosing to be sober so hard to believe? "Drinking isn't required to be a cowboy."

She *looked him up and down. "Seems muscles and a decent pair of chaps aren't either."*

*Your writing probably won't be as repetitive as the first example, but you'll be surprised by the lack of different sentence structures you can find nestled between dialogue or interior monologue that starts with 'He' and 'She.'

Hint for the Search:

I highlight 'she' and 'he' in two different colors and capital 'She' and 'He' in a different shade of the same color to scan for huge clumps of the same word while also differentiating the case. I'll also highlight the names of my hero and heroine when I do this search to check if I've clumped together a lot of sentences starting with the characters' names, since it's essentially repeating the same structure as the 'He' and 'She' sentences.

To only find the names of your main point of view characters at the beginning of sentences, you'll need to search for their individual names as indicated below:

^pName (the ^p indicates a paragraph start)

. Name

! Name

and

? Name

Make sure you put a single space between the end punctuation and the name in the find and replace box (since there should only be one space at the end of a sentence, not two).

CHAPTER 3

GRAMMAR WEASEL WORDS

ADVERB WEASELS

Adverbs are the tool of the lazy writer.

MARK TWAIN

RAISE your hand if you remember an elementary teacher instructing you to make your writing more descriptive and colorful by adding adjectives and adverbs (see terms).

Yeah, don't always listen to the teacher in your head from days gone past. I should know—I was one! Back when I taught high school English, I could hardly make myself assign creative writing because I had no idea how to write fiction, and I knew it. English teachers can dissect a piece, but creating one is a different story.

-ly

The reason why –*ly* adverbs are weasel words is because they are often unneeded or redundant. If they are needed, they're often telling instead of showing.

Examples of unneeded or redundant adverbs:

> *He jumped up and down, clapping **excitedly**. "I'm going to be a big brother!"*
>
> *He sprinted **quickly** toward town.*

*These adverbs are redundant. The boy's action of jumping and clapping show readers he's excited, and sprinting, by definition, is quick. Eliminate these –*ly* verbs.

Examples of adverbs acting as a crutch for a weak verb:

> Example: *He entered the room **quietly**.*
>
> Fix: *He slipped into the room.*
>
> Example: *She moved the chair **forcefully**.*
>
> Fix: *She shoved the chair.*

* Choose a stronger verb to eliminate these adverbs.

Example of an adverb telling what you should show:

> Example: *He looked up at her **sadly**.*
>
> Fix: *He looked up at her, his eyes dark and wet.*

*'Sadly' seems to be a necessary adverb since you can't pick a better verb and eliminating it changes the meaning of the sentence, but this adverb is "lazy writing" (as Mark Twain put

it). It'll take more work for the writer to show what this adverb tells, but that's what needs to happen.

Yes, this will add to word count. Getting rid of weasel words is not always about word count reduction. Sometimes it's about improving the writing.

Example of an adverb that tells what dialogue and action should show:

> Example: *"Come over here,"* she said **suggestively**.
>
> Fix: *"Come over here, big boy." She gave him a wink before turning. Her hips swayed as she walked toward the bar.*

If you want to make sure your reader knows how your character is saying something in a particular manner (e.g. sadly, angrily, flirtatiously, fearfully), your dialogue needs to be written to show that on its own. If the reader can't tell how the character is saying something without an adverb, you either need to rewrite the dialogue, put in action beats (see terms), or do both.

Hint for the Search:

Word can search for suffixes by checking the "match suffix" box. Open Office and Scrivener don't have this feature, but if you leave "whole word" unchecked it will highlight all words with *-ly* in it. This will pick up more than suffixes, but will still help you find *–ly* adverbs. You can check the "match case" box so you can eliminate some words that start with 'ly' from your search.

PREPOSITION WEASELS

Certain actions assume a preposition (see terms) without needing to write the preposition, and are therefore redundant. These unneeded prepositions are used in more than the example phrases below, but they'll demonstrate why these prepositions are well-known word count fillers.

across, around, back, down, off, out, over, up

stood, climbed (**up**)

sat (**down**)

looked/glanced (**back**) over shoulder

spun (**around**)

went (**off**) to

crossed his/her arms (**across**, **over** chest)

stooped/bent/crouched (**down**)

reached/shouted (**out**)

One thing you'll notice when searching for prepositions is that you can't remove them when they are part of a phrasal verb (see terms), though you could swap them out for non-phrasal verbs:

Example: *He stepped **down** from the position.*

*'down' in this instance is part of a phrasal verb. You can swap

'stepped down' for another verb like 'resigned' but if you've already used 'resigned' in a nearby sentence, you might want to keep this phrasal verb to avoid an echo, even if 'resigned' would tighten the sentence.

of

The preposition 'of' likes to eat up your word count when it's used in a possessive phrase. This may not be a big deal, but if you're looking to reduce your word count, getting rid of wordy ways to say things is a good way to tighten.

> Example: *He couldn't remember the names **of** the children.*
>
> Fix: *He couldn't remember the children's names.*
>
> Example: *He tapped his desk, signaling the end **of** the interview.*
>
> Fix: *He tapped his desk, signaling the interview's end.*

HOMOPHONES & CONFUSING WORD SET WEASELS

There are too many homophone pairs for it to be worthwhile to highlight every single homophone in your manuscript. One person's confusing word pair is not another's. If you know of your own personal difficulty with a word pair, it would be easy to add to your own personal list of bugaboos to check. Even if you know the difference between a pair, if you've caught yourself using the wrong one once, put them on the list and double check.

Pairs I catch writers mishandling often, or I've used incorrectly and had an editor correct me, are:

accept/except, adverse/averse, affect/effect, beside/besides, blonde/blond, breath/breathe, compared to/compared with, conscience/conscious, ensure/insure, farther/further, heal/heel, lay/laid/lain/lie, loath/loathe, mantle/mantel, principle/principal, rack/wrack, regard/regards, reign/rein, sail/sale, sight/site, sights/sites, stationary/stationery, undo/undue, whoever/whomever

It wouldn't hurt to check out lists of confusing word pairs and look for those that might cause you problems. The two sites below have extensive lists, along with definitions to see if you know the difference:

Words That Are Often Confused:

http://labarker.com/WritingRelated/words.html

English for Students: Homonyms:

http://www.english-for-students.com/Homonyms.html

Also, my editor told me she keeps an eye out for 'try and' instead of 'try to' in historical novels since 'try and' is a modern colloquial phrase. If you're a historical writer and find yourself using words that are too modern, you might consider making a list of those to highlight as well. (See my Seekerville blog post, *Don't Put Yourself Up a Creek Unless You Should*, for more information on finding word and phrase histories.)

it's, its; their, they're, there; whose, who's; your, you're

I also suggest checking your pronoun homonym sets, even if you know them well. We've all seen people get them wrong, and once you write the wrong version, it's as if they turn invisible during the next read through. I find several wrong in my manuscripts even though I know the differences.

You can also look for an apostrophe 's' ('s) to check for incorrect usage/typos that won't get picked up by a grammar check:

Example: *She drove to her parent **'s** home.*

*This could be right if she was going to the home of one of her parents because they live separately, but it's wrong if her parents live together. Instead it would need to be a plural possessive (parents').

DANGLING AND MISPLACED MODIFIER WEASELS

There are three reasons to check words ending with *–ing*, especially when used at the beginning of a sentence. In this section, we'll deal with dangling and misplaced modifiers. We'll deal with the Progressive Weasels in the next section.

-ing

It's easy to start sentences with a dangling or misplaced modifiers in the quest to vary sentence structures. They can occur in other parts of the sentence too, but the beginning is the most common.

Dangling Modifier:

Example: *Be**ing** consumed with guilt, the ice cream made her feel better.*

A modifier should modify the subject of the clause (see terms) it's attached to, but ice cream isn't capable of feeling guilty. If the –*ing* phrase is not describing the noun it's attached to, it's considered a dangling modifier. To fix it, you need to make sure the modifier grammatically attaches to the right subject.

Fix: *Be**ing** consumed with guilt, Lily shoveled in a spoonful of ice cream. At least sugar and cream made her feel a little better.*

Better Fix (see reasoning in the Emotion-Naming Weasels section): *Lily took one bite of ice cream and sank against the counter. If only the comfort of sugar and cream could erase the sins she'd committed today.*

Misplaced Modifier:

Example: *Run**ning** across the football field, Mary handed the quarterback his ball.*

A misplaced modifier happens when a verb phrase modifying a noun can't happen simultaneously with the action of the sentence it's attached to. Mary can't hand a ball to the quarterback the entire time she's running across the field.

Fix: *After run**ning** across the football field, Mary handed the quarterback his ball.*

Or

Mary ran across the football field and handed the quarterback his ball.

Hint for the Search:

I would not run this search by itself. I combine my search for *-ing* to catch dangling and misplaced modifiers along with the Progressive Weasels which I address next.

CHAPTER 4

TO BE WEASEL WORDS

'WAS' and other 'to be' verbs can be acceptably used hundreds of times in a book. However, they often indicate something could be written tighter or deeper. Some people have asked me why 'was' is considered a weasel word when you can't simply eliminate it from a sentence. But it's not that 'was' isn't grammatically necessary for the sentence. Rather it's an indicator that you are telling or could tighten your writing.

Searching out 'to be' verbs can help you find four different problems. I'll address three in this section: progressive, expletive, and passive weasels.

PRESENT/PAST PROGRESSIVE WEASELS

was, were, be, been, –ing

One type of 'to be' weasel occurs with verbs ending in *–ing*. When you find this present progressive or past progressive verb construction, it is often best to tighten the verb tense to simple present or simple past. The progressive tense often sounds as if you're telling the reader a story rather than letting them experience it. But don't eliminate progressive verbs without thought. If the action needs to be progressive, keep it that way.

> Example: *I **was** sitt**ing** on the stoop, watching people go by.*
>
> Fix: *I sat on the stoop, watching people go by.*
>
> Example: *The hutch was entirely too small for the rabbit he'd **be** bring**ing** home later.*
>
> Fix: *The hutch was entirely too small for the rabbit he'd bring home later.*
>
> Example: *He **was** read**ing** a magazine when she came in.*
>
> Cannot become: *He read a magazine when she came in.*

*This is an example of when to keep the progressive tense since the meaning changes if rewritten.

Hint for the Search:

For this search, I highlight the 'to be' verbs in one color and the *–ing* suffix in another, enabling me to scan through the manuscript and see where these two colors are close together to check for verb tense problems in those spots.

EXPLETIVE WEASELS

In grammar, an expletive is a word that serves a function, but has no meaning. They're useless and can almost always be eliminated. Technically, many weasel words in this book could be considered Expletive Weasels, but in this section, I'm concentrating on these expletive phrases:

it was, there was (were), there would be, what . . . was/were

Example: ***There is*** *no way I'd ever get a date with her.*

Fix: *I had no chance of getting a date with her.*

Example: ***There were*** *feathers floating all around.*

Fix: *Feathers floated all around.*

Example: ***There would be*** *hundreds of people at the football game.*

Fix: *Hundreds of people would attend the football game.*

Example: ***It is*** *a cool day in October.*

Fix: *The day is cool for October.*

Example: ***It was*** *the onions that made him cry.*

Fix: *The onions made him cry.*

Example: ***What*** *he wanted* ***was*** *her love.*

Fix: *He wanted her love.*

*When you've buried a subject in a subordinate clause (the 'what . . . was' being the expletive), rewrite it as a main clause.

An example of an expletive construction that doesn't necessarily need to be fixed:

Example: *Sewing calms me.* ***It is*** *the only thing that keeps me from crying.*

*You shouldn't fix this one by replacing 'it' with its antecedent (see terms) since you'd create an echo by repeating the word 'sewing.' However, to avoid a vague 'it' (which will be talked about in the Vague Weasels section) or to add color/texture to your writing, you should check if replacing 'it' with something more specific will improve things, such as:

Fix: *Sewing calms me. The constant passing of the needle through fabric keeps me too busy to cry.*

PASSIVE BE WEASELS

was, were, being, been, by

Most people have heard of making your sentences active instead of passive. Searching out 'to be' verbs and the word 'by' can help you find instances where you may have written a passive sentence construction.

Example: *He **was** eaten **by** zombies.*

Fix: *Zombies ate him.*

Example: *One of the girls **was** hit in the face **by** John's flailing arms.*

Fix: *John's flailing arms hit one of the girls in the face.*

Example: *I **was** still gett**ing** knocked around by the steady stream of students, so I moved closer to the wall.*

Fix: *The steady stream of students knocked me around, so I moved closer to the wall.*

Example: *The song **was being** played out of tune.*

Fix: *George winced as the fiddler screeched out a long, awful note on his poorly tuned instrument.*

*This example is a passive construction where the 'by' part of the sentence was left off. (You could write "by the fiddle player" at the end of the sentence to see that it is indeed passive.) However, I did not simply flip the sentence from passive to active by naming the player since the player is not important to the scene.

But I did rewrite it in an active structure to highlight who is important to the scene—the character being affected by the setting detail. Making the setting interact or show something about the character is one way to enhance the fictive dream and write in deeper point of view.

If it isn't important to know who or what is doing the action, you might choose to keep a passive construction. For example, you might choose to keep the passive construction if the doer is unknown, unwanted, unneeded, or if you want to highlight the action over the doer. But think through switching it to active to see if it helps enliven your scene before deciding against it.

Hint for the Search:

For this search, I highlight 'to be' verbs in one color and 'by' in another, enabling me to quickly find where they are close together and check for this specific problem.

CHAPTER 5

VAGUE AND CONFUSING WEASEL WORDS

VAGUE WEASELS

WHEN WRITING, we want to make sure everything is clear to the reader.

it, something, stuff, that, thing

In your manuscript, highlight 'it' to see if every instance of 'it' has a clear antecedent (see terms). But even if your 'it' isn't vague, 'it' is a visually deficient word. Replacing 'it' with a more descriptive alternative gives depth to your setting or story.

Example of a vague 'it':

> Example: *She snatched her paper and pen back from him, then stuffed **it** into her disorganized folder.*
>
> Fix: *She snatched her paper and pen back from him, then stuffed the fancy stationery into her disorganized folder.*

Example: ***It*** *wasn't what I was hoping for. I was supposed to see fireworks and feel heart bubbles popping.*

Fix: *I was supposed to see fireworks when he got down on one knee, but not even one happy heart bubble popped off inside me.*

Example: *George stared at the wall.* ***It was*** *covered with sauce.*

Fix: *George stared at the wall. The faded green wallpaper was covered with sauce.*

*The 'it' in the last example clearly referred to the wall, but readers were robbed of a visual and left with an empty placeholder word.

Example of problems with a vague 'something,' 'stuff,' 'that,' or 'thing:'

Example: *He skirted the **stuff** in the hallway as he ran after the perp.*

Fix: *He skirted the mannequins, broken set pieces, and theater curtains piled in the hallway as he chased the perp.*

Example: *She brought all her **things** to the party.*

Fix: *She brought every piece of Tupperware she owned to the party.*

Don't let vague weasel words steal visuals from your reader's fictive dream—but balance this against pacing (see terms).

Hint for the Search:

I search for these weasels at the same time I search for the Vague Action Weasels below.

VAGUE ACTION WEASELS

Sometimes certain verbs are not needed or weak. Common verbs that should be searched out to avoid this problem:

came, entered, looked, found, saw, stood (there), sat (there), made, moved, turned, walked, went

> Example: *He **stood there** waiting for the phone to ring.*
>
> Fix: *He waited for the phone to ring.*
>
> Example: *He **looked** over at the children playing in the park.*
>
> Fix: *Children played in the park.*

*We'll assume your POV character is looking, because if he can describe something visual, he is indeed looking. If he can't see something, he shouldn't be describing it (unless he's doing so from memory).

> Example: *He **moved** across the room to get the papers.*
>
> Fix: *He retrieved the papers from the desk.*

*Readers will assume he moved without being told.

TIMING WEASELS

To make the fictive dream easy to follow, things should happen chronologically. Writing events and reactions out of order forces your reader to back up to correct the timeline of the movie playing in their head. You want your reader to live in the dream right along with the characters without having to stop to rearrange the story in their mind.

The following words can help you catch if you've written actions and reactions out of order. These timing weasels may not sniff out all your timing problems, but it's a nice place to start.

after, before, later, since, when

Example: *He sighed **after** she left the room.*

Fix: ***After** she left the room, he sighed.*

Example: ***Before** walking farther into the cave, he glanced down at her.*

Fix: *He glanced down at her, then walked farther into the cave.*

Example: *She pulled away from him **since** he'd pinched her.*

Fix: *He pinched her, so she pulled away.*

Example: *She screamed **when** he hit her.*

Fix: *He hit her. She screamed.*

Example: *He'd realize **later** that he'd left his keys.*

*This last one can't be fixed at this point in the story because it's author intrusion (see terms). If the character doesn't know he's left his keys behind, the reader can't either. Instead, wait until later in the story to write: "Ugh! Where are my keys?"

CHAPTER 6

POV-DISTANCING WEASEL WORDS

WRITING in deep point of view (deep POV) is writing so readers feel as if they are living through a story rather than being told a story. Readers often find stories more enjoyable if they feel as if they are "wearing the skin" of your point-of-view character.

If you are unfamiliar with deep POV, you can Google articles about it. The ebooks, *Riveting your Readers with Deep Point of View by Jill Elizabeth Nelson* or *Understanding Show, Don't Tell by Janice Hardy*, are nice primers on the subject.

The following weasel word groups will often alert you to when you've written shallow POV instead of deep POV, aka Telling vs. Showing.

DIALOGUE TAG WEASELS

asked, barked, exclaimed, ground out, growled, murmured, mused, questioned, responded, said, shouted

Most writing instructors will tell you not to use these different dialogue tags and will often declare that the word 'said' is invisible, so when using dialogue tags, they suggest you use nothing but "said." They are correct that using creative dialogue tags is annoying:

Example:

"Hello," she **said**.

"Hi," he **responded**, *setting down his phone.*

"Want to go out sometime?" she **questioned**.

"Of course," **he murmured**.

However, replacing all those dialogue tags with 'said' will not make this scene better. No dialogue tag enhances the story world. The fact that words are in quotes means the reader already knows someone said or asked something, so dialogue tags are often useless for anything other than marking who's speaking.

Save 'said' and 'asked' (the two most basic dialogue tags), for fast-paced scenes or scenes with lots of characters. When not writing such scenes, try to use action beats (see terms) or interior monologue (see terms) to indicate who's speaking while also enhancing the story world for your readers.

Fix:

"Hello."

The footsteps coming toward him stopped. He glanced up.

Mary.

"Hi." *He set down his phone and sighed.*

> "Want to go out sometime?" Her eyes sparked, warning him of the fury she'd unleash should he attempt to say no.
>
> "Of course." What other option did he have? She'd spill his secret if he didn't keep her happy.

I do find a few dialogue tags to be useful on occasion, such as 'muttered' and 'whispered,' since an action beat to indicate these often adds nothing of value to the scene.

LINKING VERB WEASELS

was, were, appeared, became, felt, grew, looked, remained, seemed, sounded, stayed

When a verb connects a subject to a predicate nominative or predicate adjective (see terms), it works as a linking verb. Using linking verbs seems to be a nice, non-wordy way to write. However, it often indicates you've told something you could have shown. Though showing will almost always add to your word count, showing instead of telling enhances the fictive dream.

> Example: He **was** beat.
>
> Fix: He slumped in his chair, his head hitting the headrest with a thump.
>
> Example: She **was** beyond ill.
>
> Fix: Her head swam, and she could barely stand. With a hand over her eyes, she blocked out the light, which only intensified the stabbing pain between her brows.

Example: *She **appeared** tipsy.*

Fix: *The woman's giggle slurred and her head lolled to the side. She gave him a smile that looked painful, before hiccuping and grabbing her half-empty mug.*

Example: *The farther he walked, the weaker he **seemed** to **grow**.*

Fix: *With each step, his joints protested. He needed to sit. Soon. He arrived at the bench just as his legs buckled.*

Linking Verb Weasels can also be worthless placeholders. Consider moving predicate adjectives or nominatives (see terms) to another place in the sentence, and use a powerful verb instead.

Example: *The dress she wore **was** red.*

Fix: *Her red dress ruffled in the breeze.*

Example: *I sat in the lobby which **was** full of people.*

Fix: *I sat in the crowded lobby.*

Example: *The sun **was** an orb of fire.*

Fix: *The sun, an orb of orange-red fire, beat down upon the earthlings.*

Hint for the Search:

I combine the Linking Verb weasel search with the two following groups of weasel words: Shallow POV Weasels and Emotion Naming Weasels.

SHALLOW POV WEASELS

To write in deep POV (see terms), you show the story instead of tell it. If you find a POV distancing weasel in your manuscript, you've likely written something in shallow POV.

appeared, believed, considered, decided, heard, feared, feeling, guess(ed)(ing), idea, knew, looked, memories, mind, noticed, prayed, prayer, question(s)(ing), realized, recognized, resolution, resolved, respected, saw, seemed, smelled, supposed, suspected, thought(s), touched, understood, wanted, watched, wondered, wish(ed)(ing), without thinking, without thought

Most people don't think, "I've decided to eat popcorn." They simply decide. You don't think about looking at things. You simply see what you are looking at. So when you write a scene in a certain character's POV, you don't need to mention that they looked or decided. Instead, you write about what they looked at or decided upon. This keeps the fictive dream rolling.

However, you usually don't have to eliminate these weasel words when your POV character is thinking about another character doing these things. In real life, it's natural to realize "The girl across the table is looking at me funny" or "The nurse prayed as if my life depended upon it."

Fixing Shallow POV weasels can be difficult. You may be tempted to leave them as is, but you're gypping your reader out of a deeper experience. Eliminating these weasel words may take more words, but readers prefer better storytelling over smaller word count.

Example: He **believed** her.

Fix: *He looked into her glistening eyes, brimming with real tears. She couldn't have murdered that man. Couldn't have. Plain and simple.*

*The example sentence would have been fine if the sentence was in the heroine's POV and she's realizing the hero believed her. 'He believed her' would be a thought she'd have about someone else, but could still use some expansion. But if this is interior monologue in the hero's POV, then it is telling instead of showing.

Example: *She **thought** to try the other key just in case.*

Fix: *Hadn't she tried them all? She flipped the keys around the ring. The skeleton key looked too big for the lock, but it wouldn't hurt to try.*

*Your POV characters shouldn't think about their thinking or 'think to themselves.' They should just think.

Example: *A look of contempt crossed Gabby's face, a face I **noticed** was now puffy on one side.*

Fix: *A look of contempt crossed Gabby's face, now slightly puffy on one side.*

Example: *The broken lock **appeared** to be some sort of clue.*

Fix: *He turned the broken lock over in his hand. Was this a clue?*

Example: *Man! How I **wished** I hadn't been so quick to stop Madeline's flirting.*

Fix: *Man! If I hadn't been so quick to stop Madeline's flirting, none of this would've happened.*

Example: She **prayed** a **prayer** for strength.

Fix: *Oh, Lord, give me strength!*

Example: *The gentleman stood upon her entrance, though it* ***seemed*** *he didn't want to acknowledge her presence.*

Fix: *The gentleman stood upon her entrance, but his lips were little more than a flat line and his body was as tight as an archer's string. The moment she sat, he flopped back into his chair with less grace than a turkey shot from the sky.*

Example: *They* ***saw*** *the horses coming at them at the same time.*

Fix: *"Do you see—?" Words failed her as the stampeding horses turned the corner and headed straight for them. She turned to look at her brother. His face had drained of color.*

Example: *She* ***hoped*** *God would deliver her.*

Fix: *She struggled to gain a breath. If God didn't save her now, she'd be seeing His face within the hour. Amelia yanked against the arm crushing her throat. God couldn't be calling her home now, not with little Emmy still in Dr. Evil's clutches.*

Example: *She* ***knew*** *he'd not shoot her.*

Fix: *He wouldn't shoot her. She stepped forward, keeping her gaze fixed on his eyes and not on the gun he held.*

Example: *I **looked** at the screen to see a lady screaming at some skinny, unshaven man who was supposedly her baby's daddy.*

Fix: *On the television screen, a lady screamed at some skinny, unshaven man who was supposedly her baby's daddy.*

Example: *He **wondered** if he'd ever be able to love again.*

Fix: *He wiped away the tears. Would he ever be able to love again?*

Example: ***Thoughts** and **memories** swirled about in her **mind** as she held the ornament. The intense **emotions** bubbling up within her kept her from thanking Mamaw.*

Fix: *She hugged the ornament to her chest, unable to form the words necessary to thank Mamaw for dragging it down from wherever it had lay hidden in the attic these past ten years. How she had laughed the day Papa had given her this reindeer ornament with its misshapen horn. If only she could snuggle into his lap once again and smell his spicy, exotic hair tonic that had always made her think he was a pirate, rather than the dock worker he claimed to be.*

Example: ***Without thinking**, he reached out to touch his lips to hers.*

Fix: *Somehow, in the space of a butterfly's breath, his lips landed upon hers.*

*Mentioning that your POV character acts without thinking takes the reader out of the character's head and into the author's, because the only person in the story who can know there are no thoughts in a character's head is the author. This takes you into the realm of omniscient POV, where the narrator is someone other than the characters on the page.

EMOTION-NAMING WEASELS

Whenever you find an emotion that is named in your manuscript, check if it distances your reader from your character by telling rather than showing the emotion. It's strange to think that naming emotions is emotionally distancing, but this is the principle of showing vs. telling.

It is fine to have your POV character guess at another character's emotions by naming it since they're not feeling the emotion themselves, but it is telling to name your POV character's emotion. Adults don't think "I'm angry." We just are.

affection, anger, angry, angst, anxiety, anxious, certain, concern, confidence, confident, courage, curiosity, curious, depressed, despair, determination, disbelief, disdain, distress, doubt, dread, elated, elation, emotions, excited, excitement, fear, foolish, foolishness, frantic, frustrated, frustration, frustrations, glad, happy, hope, hurt, joy, mirth, nervous, pain, panic, pleased, rage, regret, relieved, relief, satisfied, scared, shock, sorrow, surprise, sure, uncertain, upset, worry, worried

Example: *I **was** taken **by surprise**.*

Fix: *His arms grabbed me about the middle, and my heart jumped clean up into my throat.*

Example: *He was so **angry** at his father he could spit.*

> Fix: *How dare Father! He clenched his fists and resisted the urge to spit on Father's alligator shoes.*

*Note the change of 'his father' to 'Father.' In deep POV, your POV character will not think of relatives as their mother or uncle, but by the name they call the person.

> Example: ***Despair*** *flooded her.*
>
> Fix: *She fell to her knees. Though the ground stopped her from going any farther, her soul continued to sink, as if it could drag her down to the coffin below.*
>
> Example: *His kiss made her heart float with **hope**.*
>
> Fix: *His lips left hers, and she leaned against him to steady herself. He loved her! Even if Momma refused to see her again, she'd manage to get through this trial with Levi at her side.*
>
> Example: *"That's so much better." She sighed in **relief**.*
>
> Fix: *She sighed. "That's so much better."*

*Sometimes you should trust what you've already written to get across the emotion without using the word.

> Example: *The young deacon's glare stopped her from accepting the turkey the reverend was offering her. Did Brother Tate **hate** her so much he'd deny her food?*

*No fix is needed. The sentence above is a fine use of an emotion word because the POV character is observing someone else's emotion and naming it in her thoughts. In real life, you might think, "Boy, he hates me." But you don't often think, "I feel hate." You simply feel the effects of having the emotion.

CONCLUSION

I hope you've learned some useful ways to self-edit and strengthen your story by identifying and eliminating weasel words. If I've missed any weasel words you believe should be included on one of these lists, feel free to let me know of them, and I may add them in updates.

The following pages contain instructions on how to set up your writing software to find all these weasel words with just one click of a button.

PART 2

SETTING UP YOUR SOFTWARE TO FIND WEASEL WORDS

Now that we've gone over the different types of weasel words, it's probably daunting to think about finding and checking so many, especially in a lengthy manuscript. If the thought is overwhelming, don't convince yourself that editing with weasel words is an exercise that will drive you crazy. You don't have to do them all at once.

If you're a new writer, consider working on one weasel word writing problem at a time. Perhaps you want to concentrate on teaching yourself how to write in deep POV. So focus on editing with the POV distancing weasel words and forget about the rest until you have a handle on deep POV. Perhaps you're more concerned with proofreading your manuscript. If so, focus on editing with the grammar weasels.

Or, instead of editing an entire manuscript with all the weasel words, edit a chapter at a time (this is what I do).

And definitely don't despair over the thought of the physical aspect of having to find each and every one of these words. I'm going to teach you how to highlight a group of weasel words with just one click of a button. To make it easier, you can buy the coding from me if you prefer.

The best way to highlight an entire list of weasel words is to build a macro in Word or Open Office or a template in Scrivener. You might be wondering what a macro or a template is, but don't worry. I'll teach you.

If you are a visual person and want to watch me demonstrate how to set up macros and templates, you'll find video tutorials on the webpage for this book on my website. Be prepared to spend several hours setting this up. Not because it's difficult, but because it's time consuming.

However, once done, you'll have nothing to do but tweak your lists in the years ahead. The Scrivener template takes the least amount of time to create, and Word takes the longest. However, Word is handier because of the degree to which you can fine-tune the search. Expect to spend two to four hours if you're setting up a macro in Word, and less time if you're using a different program.

If you don't want to spend the hours setting things up and are happy with the words I have in the lists, purchasing my codes or template will get you up and running within minutes.

To purchase a pre-made code or template, skip to Part III

The following chapters contain directions for Microsoft Word 2016, Open Office 4.1.3, and Scrivener 1.9.7.0 for Windows. You may have to adjust for other versions.

Word's Instructions are found in Chapter 7.

Open Office's Instructions are found in Chapter 8.

Scrivener's Instructions are found in Chapter 9.

CHAPTER 7

SETTING UP WORD TO FIND WEASEL WORDS

IN WORD, the best way to search for a specific list of words is to build a macro. Once it's set up, you won't have to do it again. (If you happen to change computers or reinstall Word, use the instructions on how to paste in the code you could purchase from me to install your own code into your new version or computer.)

SETTING UP A MACRO:

1. In Word, go to the View tab. To the far right is a button labeled "Macros." Click the down arrow and choose "Record Macro."

2. Give your list a name that will help you remember what it's intended to help you find. (Word will not accept a macro name with a space.) I've personally named my macros the same as the sections in this book e.g. "PronounClusterWeasels" or "LinkingVerbWeasels."

3. Under "Assign macro to" you can decide to make a quick

access button that will show up above Word's menu or create a keyboard shortcut. I don't do this because you have to hover over the buttons to see what they are or memorize the buttons/shortcuts for each weasel word list. I don't find it saves time unless you intend to memorize them.

4. Leave "All Documents" in the "Store macro in:" blank so you can use this macro in any document you open in Word. In the description box, you can type something to remind you of what writing problems the particular weasel word list indicates, but it's not required.

5. Click "OK." Now your mouse arrow icon has a tiny cassette attached to it. This means Word is recording all your keystrokes and commands so it can repeat the sequence any time you run this macro, so try not to mess up! If you do, stop recording, delete the macro, and start again.

Don't type anything into the text while recording, otherwise Word will type those words into your manuscript every time you run that macro.

To highlight your list of weasel words, you can't simply find the words with the find function, you have to replace them. Otherwise, they'll disappear once you decide to fix one. Here are the commands you need to record to find and highlight all your weasel words:

1) Click the Home tab.

2) On the far-right side, click "Replace."

3) In the "Find what" box, write the first word you want to find, e.g. *was*

4) Click the "More" button on the bottom left of the pop-up box. Depending on what weasel word you are looking for, you may want to check the box for "Find whole words only," "Match suffix," or "Match case." If you previously had "Find whole words only" checked, make sure Word doesn't uncheck it after you search for a phrase. If it does, you will need to recheck "Find whole words only" when searching for a single word after searching for the phrase.

5) In the "Replace with" box, write the same word you wrote in the "Find what" box, e.g. *was*

6) Keep your cursor in the "Replace with" box, and go to the bottom left of your expanded pop-up box. Click "Format" and click "Highlight." Now look in your Home ribbon above your document and see what color your highlighting tool is set to. This is the color your macro will use, so make sure your highlighter is not set to blank. If you want a different color for this word, choose your preferred color before going to step 7.

7) Click "Replace All," then Click on "OK" in the pop-up box that tells you they've all been replaced.

8) Do 3–7 again for each word on your list.

9) Once you've inputted all the words in your list, click "Close."

10) Return to the View tab, click the down arrow under your macro button, then click "Stop Recording."

You have now built your macro. Word will now be able to search your manuscript and highlight these words with a click of a button.

To check if the macro works properly, click the down arrow under your macro button again and choose "View Macros."

You will now see your macro (it will be in a list if you've recorded more than one). Click the one you want to test and click "Run."

After your macro runs, make sure it highlights the list of words you want highlighted. If nothing is highlighted, you probably forgot to make sure a color in the highlighter box was selected, so the macro has highlighted your words with nothing.

If things did not go as planned, click on "View Macros" again, click on the one you messed up, click "Delete," then go through the process to record that macro again.

(If you'd like to skip doing this all by hand, you can buy my coding, then paste the code in to be up and running in minutes. There are directions below in the Word Macro Shortcut section to help you adjust the purchased coding if desired.)

WORD MACRO SHORTCUT:

If you feel comfortable changing code, you can shorten the recording process by cutting and pasting code.

Start by recording a macro as per the instructions above for several words or phrases that will set the formatting for any words you still need to enter. Click the down arrow of your Macro Command Box, and stop recording.

Now, choose "View Macros," click on the macro you recorded, and click "Edit."

You will now see the macro's coded instructions. Word will

skip down to the section that contains the code for the macro you requested to edit.

You then need to find the chunk of code that is specific to an individual word within that macro.

For the find-and-replace highlighting macros that I'm describing in this book, the coding starts with "With Selection.Find" and goes to "Selection.Find.Execute Replace:=wdReplaceAll" for an individual word.

The command series for an individual word looks like this:

```
With Selection.Find
.Text = "was"
.Replacement.Text = "was"
.Forward = True
.Wrap = wdFindContinue
.Format = True
.MatchCase = False
.MatchWholeWord = True
.MatchWildcards = False
.MatchSoundsLike = False
.MatchAllWordForms = False
End With
Selection.Find.Execute
    Replace:=wdReplaceAll
```

Copy the entire bit of code for one word.

Then, right after the end of this section of code, click your mouse to insert your cursor, click the enter key to give you a space to paste the code you just copied, then paste in the copied code.

Now you'll have a new line of command for Word, but you'll want this command to highlight a different word. Look for the two occurrences of 'was' in the above code. (Your code will contain whatever word the command coding you copied was for). Change both instances of 'was' to the next word on your list. Note that all words you paste in will highlight with the same color you chose for the word you copied when you first recorded the macro.

Repeat pasting in that code and changing the two words to the next ones on your list until you're finished with your list.

When finished, exit by clicking on the X in the top right-hand corner of the window to close the editing screens. Word will save automatically.

USING YOUR WORD MACRO:

When editing, I prefer to deal with only a few weasel word lists at a time, but you can run as many macros together as you like.

After I've edited a chapter as much as I can on my own, I'll do my weasel word edits. This way the weasel word edit isn't overwhelming. It would be a shame to spend time editing with weasel words, then delete big sections of text, so I do my weasel word edit after I've decided my novel is ready to send to a critique partner or editor. When I've finished my weasel word edit, I do one last read through to make sure nothing I took out messed with my voice.

After you've chosen a macro and run it, you will have all the weasel words in that list highlighted in your manuscript. Fix the ones you believe need to be fixed, and leave the ones you don't want to change.

Once you're done using the weasel words to edit, go to the Home tab, go to the far right and click "Select" then "Select All" and then change the highlighter box's color to "No Color" to unhighlight all the words you didn't delete or fix.

Now you've got a clean manuscript and can either run a new macro or continue writing as normal.

Remember, there are video tutorials on my website if you'd like to watch how this is done.

CHAPTER 8

SETTING UP OPEN OFFICE TO FIND WEASEL WORDS

THE BEST WAY TO search for all the weasel words in your specific lists in Open Office is to build a macro. Once it's set up, you won't have to do it again. (If you happen to change computers or reinstall Open Office, use the instructions on how to paste in the code you could purchase from me to install the code you've created for yourself into your new version or computer.)

There are two limitations to Open Office as opposed to Word. If there is a way to mess with the code to quickly add in words that you missed during the macro recording process, I don't know how to do it beyond deleting the macro and rerecording. And Open Office can't search for suffixes. When you search for a suffix such as *–ly* or *–ing*, Open Office will highlight that combination of letters no matter where it finds it in a word. You can choose "match case" to keep from highlighting some words that start with that combination of letters.

SETTING UP AN OPEN OFFICE MACRO:

1. Open a text document in Open Office. Type all the weasel words from one list into the text document. Do this before you begin recording your macros, otherwise Open Office will type whatever words you add during recording into your manuscript every time you run the macro.

2. Click on "Tools" then "Macros" then "Record Macro." (There is now a little pop-up window that shows you are recording.) You will now be teaching Open Office every command you want it to do for this particular macro, so try not to mess up! If you do, stop recording, delete the macro, and start again.

3. Click on "Edit" then "Find & Replace."

4. Type the first word in the group of weasel words you are creating a macro for in the "Search for" box.

5. At the bottom of the "Find & Replace" box, click "Whole words only" if you want to highlight whole words. If you're searching for suffixes like *–ly* and *–ing*, leave "Whole words only" unchecked and check "Match case" to keep from highlighting some words starting with that combination of letters.

6. Click "Find All." You should now see in the text document that Open Office has highlighted the word you are searching for with a blue box. If not, figure out what step you missed.

7. Once Open Office has found the word you want, find the highlighting marker on the menu bar. Choose whichever color you want, then click the highlighter button to highlight the word you've searched for.

8. Continue steps 4–7 for each word in your list. You may

choose to color them all the same color, or you can choose different colors.

9. Once all words in that group have been highlighted, click "Close."

10. Click "Stop Recording" in the pop-up window that showed up when you started recording your macro.

11. A new pop-up box will appear, entitled "Open Office Basic Macros." Type in a title for this macro under "Macro Name." Open Office will not accept a macro name that has spaces. You could title the groups with the same titles I give them in the book, like "ClusteredPronounWeasels" or "LinkingVerbWeasels", especially if you want to follow along with the book the first few times you use these macros to edit. Note where this macro is being saved in the folders (in "Module 1"), and click "Save."

12. To test if your macro works, go to "Edit" then "Select All," and then click the down arrow next to the highlighting color and click "No Fill" to unhighlight the whole text you were just working with. Now go to "Tools" then "Macros" then "Run Macro."

13. There may be a pop-up that tells you to install a JRE. If so, click "Ok." Wait a few seconds and you will get a pop-up box entitled "Macro Selector." In the library, recall where the macro was saved in step 11 (in "Module 1"). Find it by clicking the plus button next to "My Macros," then the plus button next to the "Standard" folder, then "Module 1." You will now see your macros in the right-hand box. Select the macro you just recorded, and click "Run."

14. Your macro should do what you set it up to do, highlighting all the words quickly. If not, you'll need to delete and rerecord.

15. Repeat steps 2–11 for each weasel word group, naming each group separately.

(If you'd like to skip doing this all by hand, you can buy my coding and then paste it in to be up and running in minutes.)

SETTING UP AN OPEN OFFICE MACRO MENU BAR:

Once you have set up your macros, you won't want to drill down through the macros library each and every time you want to run a macro. Fortunately, you can make yourself a macro menu for your toolbar.

1. To make yourself a new menu item for your toolbar in Open Office, go to "Tools" then "Macros" then "Organize Macros" then "Open Office Basic."

2. Click on the first macro in your list, then click the "Assign" button. At the top right-hand corner, click "New."

3. Type "Macros" under "Menu Name" and click "OK". Now you have a new macros menu button for your toolbar.

4. You now need to add the macros you've created to this menu button. Open Office should have pushed you back to the customize pop-up box after you clicked "OK", so now "Macros" shows up in the top "Menu" box, but you'll see nothing in the bottom box. This is where you will add the macros you want to go under your new macro menu. So now click "Add."

5. In the "Add Commands" pop-up box that just appeared, scroll down in the "Categories" box until you see "Open Office Macros." Drill down in the folders as you did before when testing your macros to find them. (Click the plus button next to "My Macros," then the plus button next to the "Standard" folder, then "Module 1.")

6. Click a macro you want available under your new macro menu button and click "Add." Once you have added them all, click "Close."

7. You will then return to the "Customize" pop-up box. You will now see all the macros you added under your macro menu title. Click "OK" and then click "Close" in the last pop-up box.

At the top of your screen, you will now see "Macros" on your toolbar. When you click it, you'll see a drop-down menu of the macros you added to this menu item. Click on the one you want to run, and it will begin automatically.

USING YOUR OPEN OFFICE MACRO:

When editing, I prefer to deal with only a few weasel word lists at a time, but you can run as many macros together as you like.

After I've edited a chapter as much as I can on my own, I'll do my weasel word edits. This way the weasel word edit isn't overwhelming. It would be a shame to spend time editing with weasel words, then delete big sections of text, so I do my weasel word edit after I've decided my novel is ready to send to a critique partner or editor. When I've finished my weasel word edit, I do one last read through to make sure nothing I took out messed with my voice.

After you've chosen a macro and run it, you will have all the weasel words in that list highlighted in your manuscript. Fix the ones you believe need to be fixed, and leave the ones you don't want to change.

When you're done using the weasel words to edit, go to "Edit" then "Select All" and choose "No Fill" under the highlighter marker button to unhighlight all the words you didn't delete or fix.

Now you've got a clean manuscript and can run a new macro to highlight another set of weasel words or continue writing as normal.

Remember, there are video tutorials on my website if you'd like to watch how this is done.

CHAPTER 9

SETTING UP SCRIVENER TO FIND WEASEL WORDS

SCRIVENER HAS a few limitations you should know about before deciding to search for weasel words there instead of in Word or Open Office. If you use Scrivener along with another program (e.g. Word), you might decide it would be better to edit weasel words elsewhere.

SCRIVENER LIMITATIONS:

You can't highlight in different colors. With some weasel words, I suggest coloring different words with different colors so you can scan your manuscript to see clumps. However, Scrivener will only highlight in yellow, making the clumping of particular words harder to see.

Phrases can only be searched for individually. When a weasel word group contains a phrase, such as 'a number of,' you can either search for one word of the phrase, like 'number,' and keep in mind you're really looking for 'a number of,' or you can search for each phrase individually (which means more searches). My weasel word lists contain several phrases—and you might add more of your own—that would need to be searched for individually or as a single word.

You can't search for suffixes. Words with *–ing* and *–ly* in the middle or beginning of a word will show up in the search, so you will have to ignore them. You can choose to "match case" to get rid of a few instance of words that start with those combination of letters. (Only Word will match suffixes, Open Office has the same limitation as Scrivener in this respect.)

CREATING A SCRIVENER TEMPLATE:

1. Open a new project in whichever template you normally use to write your novels. I'm assuming most fiction writers use the Novel template under the Fiction category, so choose that if you normally do so. Create a name for your Weasel Word Novel Template such as WeaselWordNovel. This name is only a placeholder, so don't worry too much on what you name it. Then click "Create."

2. In the upper right-hand corner of Scrivener is the search box (beside the magnifying glass). Here you will type in the words from the first set of weasel words you plan to search for. Remember, you should not include phrases, either whittle the phrases down to one word or don't include them. Also, do not use commas. Instead, put a space between each word you are searching for in the group. Type in your first set of weasel words into the search box, then click the down arrow by the magnifying glass.

3. Pressing the search box's down arrow is how you will display a menu. This is how you will tell Scrivener how you want it to search for this list of words. If you want only a part

of a word, such as for the suffix, *-ing* and *–ly*, check "Any Word." If you want to only highlight complete words, check "Whole Word." Remember that Scrivener can only follow one set of commands for the entire list i.e. it can't highlight some words whole and others partially.

4. If you want the entire list to be case sensitive, click "Case Sensitive" and make sure you've capitalized or not capitalized the words in your search box appropriately.

5. Now you're going to save this search so you can use it over and over again. At the bottom of the down arrow box, click "Save Search as Collection" and a pop-up box will appear so you can name the search. You could choose to follow the names in the book, such as 'Unneeded Weasels' or whatever will remind you what this list is to help you find. Click "OK."

6. Your search is now in a tab on the left-hand side above your binder tab. To run your search in any of your project's documents, open the document you want to edit, then click on the tab of the saved search collection. Scrivener will highlight all the weasel words from that list in your viewable document.

7. Repeat steps 2–5 for all the weasel word searches you want to have available to you in every book you write.

8. Once you have all the searches saved as search collections, you can reorganize your tabs if desired. To do this, click and hold on the tab you want to move, releasing the mouse button when it's in the place you want it to be. I put the binder tab at the top. If you think you'll be consulting this Weasel Word book as you edit using the search collections, you may want to arrange the searches in the order I have them in the book.

(Hint: If you do want to put them in the same order as this book, do steps 2–5 starting with last collection in the book first.

That way you won't have to do any rearranging, since Scrivener stacks the newest collection on top.)

9. To make sure the searches work as you wish, open the scene you want to run a weasel word search in. Click on the tab of the weasel word search collection you want to run, and then all those weasel words should now highlight in your open scene.

10. To add, fix, or delete words in a saved collection, click on the collection tab you want to adjust. Go to the search box, which will now show this particular saved collection's list of words. Add, fix, or delete words as desired. Once finished, click the down arrow by the magnifying glass, click "Save Search as Collection," and rename it something other than the original name (because Scrivener will save this as a new search). Then delete the old collection using the instructions in step 11. If you want to give this newly adjusted collection the same name as the old one, delete the old collection first, then double click on the new collection's name to rename the collection. Click off when you're finished renaming the collection.

11. If you want to delete a saved collection, click on the tab you want to get rid of and click the "-" (minus) sign on the collections bar right above the tabs. Confirm you want to delete it.

(If you'd like to skip doing this all by hand, you can buy my template and import it to be up and running in minutes.)

SAVING THE TEMPLATE FOR FUTURE USE:

Once you are happy with how all your saved search collections work, you're going to save the project as a template. From now on, instead of picking the Novel Template (or whichever you normally chose) to write your books, you will pick this Weasel

Word Template, which has everything your normal choice of template contained plus the searches.

1. Go up to "File" and click "Save as Template." Rename the title to something you'll remember like "Weasel Word Novel Template." Make sure it's under the category where you want to find it (e.g. "Fiction"). Change the description if you think you'll need to jog your memory on what this template is for, then click "OK."

2. Go to File then New Project, and choose the category you placed the template in (likely "Fiction"). You will now see your new Weasel Word Template as a choice for you to use for future books.

USING YOUR SCRIVENER TEMPLATE:

When editing, I prefer to deal with only a few weasel word lists at a time, but you can run as many macros together as you like.

After I've edited a chapter as much as I can on my own, I'll do my weasel word edits. This way the weasel word edit isn't overwhelming. It would be a shame to spend time editing with weasel words, then delete big sections of text, so I do my weasel word edit after I've decided my novel is ready to send to a critique partner or editor. When I've finished my weasel word edit, I do one last read through to make sure nothing I took out messed with my voice.

After you've chosen a macro and run it, you will have all the weasel words in that list highlighted in your manuscript. Fix the ones you believe need to be fixed, and leave the ones you don't want to change.

When finished editing, simply click off the tab of the search collection you were running, either by selecting another search collection tab to run another weasel word search or clicking on your binder tab to get rid of all highlights. Now you can return to writing as normal.

Remember, there are video tutorials on my website if you'd like to watch how this is done.

PART 3

PURCHASE AND UPLOAD THE CODE OR TEMPLATE

It took me hours to create each of these macros and templates. It may take you as long or longer, depending on how familiar you are with the process. If you are happy with my lists as they are or would rather just tweak a few things on your own (in Word and Scrivener), you can purchase a copy of the macro codes or Scrivener template for two and a half US dollars. Below are the directions on what to do with your purchased code or template. Importing these codes and templates will have you up and running in a handful of minutes.

Click here if you want to purchase the Word code.

Click here if you want to purchase the Open Office code.

Go here if you want to purchase the Scrivener template.

If you cannot access these hyperlinks, you can find them on my website:

www.melissajagears.com

Instructions for uploading and using the Word macros can be found in Chapter 10.

Instructions for uploading and using the Open Office macros can be found in Chapter 11.

Instructions for uploading and using the Scrivener template can be found in Chapter 12.

CHAPTER 10

WORD MACRO CODE UPLOADING INSTRUCTIONS

CLICK here if you want to purchase the Word code.

HOW TO PASTE THE CODE INTO WORD:

1. Download the Word macro coding text file somewhere onto your computer where you'll remember where it is (e.g. "Desktop").

2. Go to your View tab in Word. At the far right you will see a box named "Macros." Click the down arrow under "Macros" then choose "View Macros"

3. Write a placeholder name in the "Macro Name" box, something like "Weasels." Click "Create."

4. You will now see a blank box with a little bit of coding that starts off this "Weasels" macro. (If you already have some macros, Word will skip down to the code of the macro you requested to edit.) Next, highlight all the code you see below. (If you already have macros be careful only to highlight what's below):

Sub weasels()
'
' weasels Macro
'
'
End Sub.

5. After you've highlighted the bold words above, go to the text file you purchased from me, select all and copy, then paste the entire Word macro coding you purchased from me on top of the above code.

6. Once you've finished pasting, click on the Xs to close out of all the editing boxes. Word will automatically save it.

USING YOUR WORD MACRO:

When editing, I prefer to deal with only a few weasel word lists at a time, but you can run as many macros together as you like.

After I've edited a chapter as much as I can on my own, I'll do my weasel word edits. This way the weasel word edit isn't overwhelming. It would be a shame to spend time editing with weasel words, then delete big sections of text, so I do my weasel word edit after I've decided my novel is ready to send to a critique partner or editor. When I've finished my weasel word edit, I do one last read through to make sure nothing I took out messed with my voice.

To find the macros you just copied and pasted into Word, go to your View tab, click on the down arrow under "Macros," and click "View Macros." You will now see a list of different weasel word groups you can search for. They were named to go along with the weasel word groups in this book for easy reference.

Click on the weasel word group you want to highlight in the box, then click "Run."

After you've chosen a macro and run it, you will have all the weasel words in that list highlighted in your manuscript. Fix the ones you believe need to be fixed, and leave the ones you don't want to change.

Once you're done using the weasel words to edit, go to the Home tab, go to the far right and click "Select," then "Select All," and change the highlighter box's color to "No Color" to unhighlight all the words you didn't delete or fix.

Now you've got a clean manuscript and can either run a new macro or continue writing as normal.

Remember, there are video tutorials on my website if you'd like to watch how this is done.

CHAPTER 11

OPEN OFFICE MACRO CODE UPLOADING INSTRUCTIONS

CLICK here if you want to purchase the Open Office code.

HOW TO PASTE THE CODE INTO OPEN OFFICE:

1. Download the Open Office macro coding file somewhere onto your computer where you'll remember where it is (e.g. "Desktop"). Unzip the file. (Right click and click "Extract all.")

2. In Open Office, open up a text document, then go to "Tools" then "Macros" then "Organize Macros" then "Open Office Basic" In the Macro name section, type something random like Weasels, it won't matter, but you need to write something so the "New" button will show up in the right-hand side of the pop-up box. Once it does, click "New."

3. If you do not have any macros, simply highlight all the coding in the box and delete it so everything is blank. If you do have macros already installed, only highlight the code "Sub Weasels End Sub" and delete that small bit of code, leaving your cursor where that code was.

3. Find the icon that looks like a sheet of paper with a green plus. If you hover over the icon it shows "Insert BASIC Source" as its title. Click that icon.

4. Once you click the "Insert BASIC Source" icon, a pop-up box appears for you to search your computer for the code file you purchased, downloaded, and unzipped. Find the unzipped file, click on the file, and then click "Open."

5. "X" out of the Macros box once all the code appears. Open Office will automatically save.

SETTING UP AN OPEN OFFICE MACRO MENU BAR:

Once you have set up your macros, you won't want to drill down through the macros library each and every time you want to run a macro. Fortunately, you can make yourself a macro menu for your toolbar.

1. To make yourself a new menu item for your toolbar in Open Office, go to "Tools" then "Macros" then "Organize Macros" then "Open Office Basic."

2. Click on the first macro in your list, then click the "Assign" button. At the top right-hand corner, click "New."

3. Type "Macros" under "Menu Name" and click "OK". Now you have a new macros menu button for your toolbar.

4. You now need to add the macros you've created to this menu button. Open Office should have pushed you back to the customize pop-up box after you clicked "OK", so now "Macros" shows up in the top "Menu" box, but you'll see nothing in the bottom box. This is where you will add the macros you want to go under your new macro menu. So now click "Add."

5. In the "Add Commands" pop-up box that just appeared, scroll down in the "Categories" box until you see "Open Office Macros" and click that. Now click the plus button next to the "My Macros" folder, then the plus button next to the "Standard" folder, then "Module 1."

6. Click a macro you want available under your new macro menu button and click "Add." Once you have added all your macros, click "Close."

7. You will then return to the "Customize" pop-up box. You will now see all the macros you added under your macro menu title. Click "OK" and then click "Close" in the last pop-up box.

At the top of your screen, you will now see "Macros" on your toolbar. When you click it, you'll see a drop-down menu of the macros you added to this menu item. Click on the one you want to run, and it will begin automatically.

USING YOUR OPEN OFFICE MACRO:

When editing, I prefer to deal with only a few weasel word lists at a time, but you can run as many macros together as you like.

After I've edited a chapter as much as I can on my own, I'll do my weasel word edits. This way the weasel word edit isn't overwhelming. It would be a shame to spend time editing with weasel words, then delete big sections of text, so I do my weasel word edit after I've decided my novel is ready to send to a critique partner or editor. When I've finished my weasel word edit, I do one last read through to make sure nothing I took out messed with my voice.

After you've chosen a macro and run it, you will have all the weasel words in that list highlighted in your manuscript. Fix the ones you believe need to be fixed, and leave the ones you don't want to change.

When you're done using the weasel words to edit, go to "Edit" then "Select All" and choose "No Fill" under the highlighter marker button to unhighlight all the words you didn't delete or fix.

Now you've got a clean manuscript and can run a new macro to highlight another set of weasel words or continue writing as normal.

Remember, there are [video tutorials on my website](#) if you'd like to watch how this is done.

CHAPTER 12

SCRIVENER TEMPLATE UPLOADING INSTRUCTIONS

CAVEAT: Buying this template will only help you search in future novels you create with this template. If you want the weasel word searches to search through your current Scrivener project, you will either have to copy and paste all your files into the new template or create the searches within your old one.

If you're willing to do the former, it might be worth purchasing, but if you want to do the latter, there is no reason to buy the template when you'll essentially be creating the template yourself and can simply follow the directions earlier in this book.

Click here if you want to purchase the Scrivener template.

HOW TO UPLOAD YOUR PURCHASED TEMPLATE INTO SCRIVENER:

1. After purchasing the Scrivener template, make sure you download the file onto your computer someplace you will

remember where you saved it (e.g. "Desktop"). Unzip the file. (Right mouse click on the zipped file and click "Extract All.")

2. Open Scrivener and click "New Project."

3. Click on "Fiction" (or whichever category under which you want to put the template).

4. In the bottom left corner of the pop-up box, click the down arrow on "Options."

5. Choose "Import Templates."

6. Find where you downloaded the template on your computer. Click on the unzipped template file, and then click "Open." The template should now show up as a choice in your Scrivener fiction templates.

7. Now that this template is one of your permanent choices, choose this template for new book projects and use it in the same way you used the "Novel" template, except now your template has the weasel word searches already programmed for you to use.

USING YOUR SCRIVENER TEMPLATE:

When editing, I prefer to deal with only a few weasel word lists at a time, but you can run as many macros together as you like.

After I've edited a chapter as much as I can on my own, I'll do my weasel word edits. This way the weasel word edit isn't overwhelming. It would be a shame to spend time editing with weasel words, then delete big sections of text, so I do my weasel word edit after I've decided my novel is ready to send to a critique partner or editor. When I've finished my weasel word edit, I do one last read through to make sure nothing I took out messed with my voice.

After you've chosen a macro and run it, you will have all the weasel words in that list highlighted in your manuscript. Fix the ones you believe need to be fixed, and leave the ones you don't want to change.

When finished editing, click off the tab of the search collection you were running, either by selecting another search collection tab to run another weasel word search, or clicking on your binder tab to get rid of all highlights so you can return to writing as normal.

Remember, there are video tutorials on my website if you'd like to watch how this is done.

WRITING CRAFT TERMS

ACTION BEAT

Description before, between, or after dialogue, describing what the speaking character is doing. An action beat is usually used instead of a dialogue tag.

Example: *"Hey!"* ***John waved as he rushed toward her.*** *"I can't believe you're already here."*

ADVERB

A word that modifies a verb, describing how the verb is being done, e.g. *knocked **rapidly**, walked **slowly**.*

ANTECEDENT

The noun referred to by a pronoun. For example, in the sentence, 'Sarah went home to get her slippers,' the antecedent to the pronoun 'her' is the noun 'Sarah.'

AUTHOR INTRUSION

When an author writes something into the story the characters cannot realistically be aware of or pens solely for the reader's benefit, e.g. describing something the point-of-view character can't know or having a character say things the other characters already know for the purpose of informing the reader. (Author intrusion can be a literary device an author chooses to use, like choosing omniscient POV or scattering funny, running joke footnotes throughout the text. But if it's not purposely and artfully done, it's jarring.)

CLAUSE

A phrase containing a noun and a verb that may or may not be able to stand alone, e.g. 'When Jim ran,' or 'Jim ran.' are both clauses.

DEEP POINT OF VIEW (DEEP POV)

Writing that helps the reader experience the story as if he or she is inside the head of the point-of-view character, living in their skin, rather than being told a story by a narrator-like voice. In deep POV, the reader is only made aware of what the scene's point-of-view character can sense, think, and feel.

ECHO

When words are used too often or too close together, making the words stick out, bringing attention to the author's word choice rather than the story.

EXPLETIVE

A word or phrase that adds no value or information.

FICTIVE DREAM

The mental movie readers imagine while reading a story, using the descriptions and details provided by the author.

HOMOPHONE

Words that are pronounced the same but have a different meaning and/or spelling, e.g. 'knot' and 'not.'

INTERIOR MONOLOGUE

The thoughts of the point-of-view character without calling attention to it being the character's thoughts, e.g. "She wished she could have gone" in third person or "I wish I could have gone" in first person instead of "'I wish I could have gone,' thought Mary."

PACING

How quickly or slowly action unfolds in a scene to set mood and tone or keep the reader's interest.

PHRASAL VERB

A verb phrase that contains a non-verb word which cannot be eliminated without changing the meaning. 'I broke into the house' is not the same as 'I broke the house.' 'Broke into' is the entire verb even though 'into' by itself is considered a preposition.

PREDICATE NOMINATIVE/ADJECTIVE

A word that comes after a linking verb that renames or describes the subject, e. g. *John is a **boy*** (where 'boy' is a predicate nominative), or *John is **funny*** (where 'funny' is a predicate adjective).

PREPOSITION

Words that show a relationship between two things, e.g. into, on, behind, down, etc.

WEASEL WORD

Words a writer can eliminate from manuscripts to tighten their writing or words that help identify writing craft problems.

ACKNOWLEDGMENTS

I want to thank Cara Grandle for pushing me to write this book and telling others about it, along with beta reading. Also many thanks to Amber Lynn Perry for beta reading and fielding oddball questions. Thanks to Naomi Rawlings and Iola Goulton for your editing and help in making this better. And to Lori Copeland for taking my crazy cover suggestions and making something slick.

ABOUT THE AUTHOR

Much to her introverted self's delight, award-winning writer **Melissa Jagears** hardly needs to leave home to be a homeschooling mother and novelist. She lives in Kansas with her husband and three children and can be found online at Facebook, Pinterest, Goodreads, and www.melissajagears.com. Feel free to drop her a note at author@melissajagears.com, or you can find her current mailing address and an updated list of her books on her website.

Get notified when Melissa has a new book release, sale, and other special events by signing up for her author newsletter at her website.

ALSO BY MELISSA JAGEARS

<u>Unexpected Brides</u>
Love by the Letter*
A Bride for Keeps
A Bride in Store
A Bride at Last

<u>Teaville Moral Society</u>
Engaging the Competition**
A Heart Most Certain
A Love So True
Tied and True***
A Chance at Forever

*e-novella. Also included in the *With All My Heart* novella collection.

**e-novella. Also include in the *With This Ring?* novella collection.

***e-novella. Also included in the *Hearts Entwined* novella collection.

© 2018 Melissa Jagears

Published by Utmost Publishing

All Rights Reserved. No part of this book may be reproduced in any form or by any electronic or mechanical means including information storage and retrieval systems without permission in writing from the author, except by a reviewer, who may quote brief passages in a review.

ISBN 978-1-948678-00-1 (Paperback Edition)

Editing by Christian Editing Services

Book Design by LC Design

Created with Vellum

www.ingramcontent.com/pod-product-compliance
Lightning Source LLC
Chambersburg PA
CBHW070032040426
42333CB00040B/1571